Great Works

Instructional Guide for Literature

To Kill a Mockingbird

A guide for the novel by Harper Lee
Great Works Author: Kristin Kemp

SHELL EDUCATION

Publishing Credits

Robin Erickson, *Production Director*; Lee Aucoin, *Creative Director*;
Timothy J. Bradley, *Illustration Manager*; Emily R. Smith, M.A.Ed., *Editorial
Director*; Amber Goff, *Editorial Assistant*; Don Tran, *Production Supervisor*;
Corinne Burton, M.A.Ed., *Publisher*

Image Credits

Cover images Maria Dryfhout/Shutterstock, Chesapeake Images/Shutterstock, Heather A. Craig/Shutterstock

Standards

© 2007 Teachers of English to Speakers of Other Languages, Inc. (TESOL)
© 2007 Board of Regents of the University of Wisconsin System. World-Class Instructional Design and Assessment (WIDA)
© Copyright 2010 National Governors Association Center for Best Practices and Council of Chief State School Officers.
All rights reserved

Shell Education

5301 Oceanus Drive
Huntington Beach, CA 92649-1030
http://www.shelleducation.com

ISBN 978-1-4258-8999-9
© 2014 Shell Educational Publishing, Inc.

Table of Contents

How to Use This Literature Guide

Today's standards demand rigor and relevance in the reading of complex texts. The units in this series guide teachers in a rich and deep exploration of worthwhile works of literature for classroom study. The most rigorous instruction can also be interesting and engaging!

Many current strategies for effective literacy instruction have been incorporated into these instructional guides for literature. Throughout the units, text-dependent questions are used to determine comprehension of the book as well as student interpretation of the vocabulary words. The books chosen for the series are complex exemplars of carefully crafted works of literature. Close reading is used throughout the units to guide students toward revisiting the text and using textual evidence to respond to prompts orally and in writing. Students must analyze the story elements in multiple assignments for each section of the book. All of these strategies work together to rigorously guide students through their study of literature.

The next few pages will make clear how to use this guide for a purposeful and meaningful literature study. Each section of this guide is set up in the same way to make it easier for you to implement the instruction in your classroom.

Theme Thoughts

The great works of literature used throughout this series have important themes that have been relevant to people for many years. Many of the themes will be discussed during the various sections of this instructional guide. However, it would also benefit students to have independent time to think about the key themes of the novel.

Before students begin reading, have them complete *Pre-Reading Theme Thoughts* (page 13). This graphic organizer will allow students to think about the themes outside the context of the story. They'll have the opportunity to evaluate statements based on important themes and defend their opinions. Be sure to have students keep their papers for comparison to the *Post-Reading Theme Thoughts* (page 64). This graphic organizer is similar to the pre-reading activity. However, this time, students will be answering the questions from the point of view of one of the characters of the novel. They have to think about how the character would feel about each statement and defend their thoughts. To conclude the activity, have students compare what they thought about the themes before they read the novel to what the characters discovered during the story.

How to Use This Literature Guide (cont.)

Vocabulary

Each teacher overview page has definitions and sentences about how key vocabulary words are used in the section. These words should be introduced and discussed with students. There are two student vocabulary activity pages in each section. On the first page, students are asked to define the ten words chosen by the author of this unit. On the second page in most sections, each student will select at least eight words that he or she finds interesting or difficult. For each section, choose one of these pages for your students to complete. With either assignment, you may want to have students get into pairs to discuss the meanings of the words. Allow students to use reference guides to define the words. Monitor students to make sure the definitions they have found are accurate and relate to how the words are used in the text.

On some of the vocabulary student pages, students are asked to answer text-related questions about the vocabulary words. The following question stems will help you create your own vocabulary questions if you'd like to extend the discussion.

- How does this word describe _____'s character?
- In what ways does this word relate to the problem in this story?
- How does this word help you understand the setting?
- In what ways is this word related to the story's solution?
- Describe how this word supports the novel's theme of . . . .
- What visual images does this word bring to your mind?
- For what reasons might the author have chosen to use this particular word?

At times, more work with the words will help students understand their meanings. The following quick vocabulary activities are a good way to further study the words.

- Have students practice their vocabulary and writing skills by creating sentences and/or paragraphs in which multiple vocabulary words are used correctly and with evidence of understanding.
- Students can play vocabulary concentration. Students make a set of cards with the words and a separate set of cards with the definitions. Then, students lay the cards out on the table and play concentration. The goal of the game is to match vocabulary words with their definitions.
- Students can create word journal entries about the words. Students choose words they think are important and then describe why they think each word is important within the novel.

How to Use This Literature Guide (cont.)

Analyzing the Literature

After students have read each section, hold small-group or whole-class discussions. Questions are written at two levels of complexity to allow you to decide which questions best meet the needs of your students. The Level 1 questions are typically less abstract than the Level 2 questions. Level 1 is indicated by a square, while Level 2 is indicated by a triangle.

These questions focus on the various story elements, such as character, setting, and plot. Student pages are provided if you want to assign these questions for individual student work before your group discussion. Be sure to add further questions as your students discuss what they've read. For each question, a few key points are provided for your reference as you discuss the novel with students.

Reader Response

In today's classrooms, there are often great readers who are below average writers. So much time and energy is spent in classrooms getting students to read on grade level, that little time is left to focus on writing skills. To help teachers include more writing in their daily literacy instruction, each section of this guide has a literature-based reader response prompt. Each of the three genres of writing is used in the reader responses within this guide: narrative, informative/explanatory, and argument. Students have a choice between two prompts for each reader response. One response requires students to make connections between the reading and their own lives. The other prompt requires students to determine text-to-text connections or connections within the text.

Close Reading the Literature

Within each section, students are asked to closely reread a short section of text. Since some versions of the novels have different page numbers, the selections are described by chapter and location, along with quotations to guide the readers. After each close reading, there are text-dependent questions to be answered by students.

Encourage students to read each question one at a time and then go back to the text and discover the answer. Work with students to ensure that they use the text to determine their answers rather than making unsupported inferences. Once students have answered the questions, discuss what they discovered. Suggested answers are provided in the answer key.

How to Use This Literature Guide *(cont.)*

Close Reading the Literature *(cont.)*

The generic, open-ended stems below can be used to write your own text-dependent questions if you would like to give students more practice.

- Give evidence from the text to support . . . .
- Justify your thinking using text evidence about . . . .
- Find evidence to support your conclusions about . . . .
- What text evidence helps the reader understand . . . ?
- Use the book to tell why _____ happens.
- Based on events in the story, ...
- Use text evidence to describe why . . . .

Making Connections

The activities in this section help students make cross-curricular connections to writing, mathematics, science, social studies, or the fine arts. Each of these types of activities requires higher-order thinking skills from students.

Creating with the Story Elements

It is important to spend time discussing the common story elements in literature. Understanding the characters, setting, and plot can increase students' comprehension and appreciation of the story. If teachers discuss these elements daily, students will more likely internalize the concepts and look for the elements in their independent reading. Another important reason for focusing on the story elements is that students will be better writers if they think about how the stories they read are constructed.

Students are given three options for working with the story elements. They are asked to create something related to the characters, setting, or plot of the novel. Students are given a choice on this activity so that they can decide to complete the activity that most appeals to them. Different multiple intelligences are used so that the activities are diverse and interesting to all students.

How to Use This Literature Guide (cont.)

Culminating Activity

This open-ended, cross-curricular activity requires higher-order thinking and allows for a creative product. Students will enjoy getting the chance to share what they have discovered through reading the novel. Be sure to allow them enough time to complete the activity at school or home.

Comprehension Assessment

The questions in this section are modeled after current standardized tests to help students analyze what they've read and prepare for tests they may see in their classrooms. The questions are dependent on the text and require critical-thinking skills to answer.

Response to Literature

The final post-reading activity is an essay based on the text that also requires further research by students. This is a great way to extend this book into other curricular areas. A suggested rubric is provided for teacher reference.

Correlation to the Standards

Shell Education is committed to producing educational materials that are research and standards based. As part of this effort, we have correlated all of our products to the academic standards of all 50 states, the District of Columbia, the Department of Defense Dependents Schools, and all Canadian provinces.

Purpose and Intent of Standards

Standards are designed to focus instruction and guide adoption of curricula. Standards are statements that describe the criteria necessary for students to meet specific academic goals. They define the knowledge, skills, and content students should acquire at each level. Standards are also used to develop standardized tests to evaluate students' academic progress. Teachers are required to demonstrate how their lessons meet standards. Standards are used in the development of all of our products, so educators can be assured they meet high academic standards.

How to Find Standards Correlations

To print a customized correlation report of this product for your state, visit our website at http://www.shelleducation.com and follow the online directions. If you require assistance in printing correlation reports, please contact our Customer Service Department at 1-877-777-3450.

Correlation to the Standards (cont.)

Standards Correlation Chart

The lessons in this guide were written to support the Common Core College and Career Readiness Anchor Standards. This chart indicates which sections of this guide address the anchor standards.

Common Core College and Career Readiness Anchor Standard	Section
CCSS.ELA-Literacy.CCRA.R.1—Read closely to determine what the text says explicitly and to make logical inferences from it; cite specific textual evidence when writing or speaking to support conclusions drawn from the text.	Close Reading the Literature Sections 1–5; Analyzing the Literature Sections 1–5; Making Connections Section 3
CCSS.ELA-Literacy.CCRA.R.2—Determine central ideas or themes of a text and analyze their development; summarize the key supporting details and ideas.	Analyzing the Literature Sections 1–5; Creating with the Story Elements Sections 3, 5; Making Connections Section 4
CCSS.ELA-Literacy.CCRA.R.3—Analyze how and why individuals, events, or ideas develop and interact over the course of a text.	Analyzing the Literature Sections 1–5; Creating with the Story Elements Sections 1–5
CCSS.ELA-Literacy.CCRA.R.4—Interpret words and phrases as they are used in a text, including determining technical, connotative, and figurative meanings, and analyze how specific word choices shape meaning or tone.	Vocabulary Sections 1–5; Making Connections Section 2
CCSS.ELA-Literacy.CCRA.R.10—Read and comprehend complex literary and informational texts independently and proficiently.	Entire Unit
CCSS.ELA-Literacy.CCRA.W.1—Write arguments to support claims in an analysis of substantive topics or texts using valid reasoning and relevant and sufficient evidence.	Analyzing the Literature Sections 1–5; Close Reading the Literature Sections 1–5; Reader Response Sections 1–5
CCSS.ELA-Literacy.CCRA.W.2—Write informative/explanatory texts to examine and convey complex ideas and information clearly and accurately through the effective selection, organization, and analysis of content.	Reader Response Sections 2, 4; Making Connections Section 1; Creating with the Story Elements Section 4; Post-Reading Response to Literature
CCSS.ELA-Literacy.CCRA.W.3—Write narratives to develop real or imagined experiences or events using effective technique, well-chosen details and well-structured event sequences.	Reader Response Sections 1, 3, 5; Making Connections Section 5; Creating with the Story Elements Sections 1–2, 5
CCSS.ELA-Literacy.CCRA.W.4—Produce clear and coherent writing in which the development, organization, and style are appropriate to task, purpose, and audience.	Reader Response Sections 1–5; Creating with the Story Elements Sections 1–2; Making Connections Section 1; Post-Reading Response to Literature
CCSS.ELA-Literacy.CCRA.W.5—Develop and strengthen writing as needed by planning, revising, editing, rewriting, or trying a new approach.	Post-Reading Response to Literature

Correlation to the Standards (cont.)

Standards Correlation Chart (cont.)

Common Core College and Career Readiness Anchor Standard	Section
CCSS.ELA-Literacy.CCRA.W.7—Conduct short as well as more sustained research projects based on focused questions, demonstrating understanding of the subject under investigation.	Analyzing the Literature Sections 1–5; Reader Response Sections 1–5; Post-Reading Response to Literature
CCSS.ELA-Literacy.CCRA.W.9—Draw evidence from literary or informational texts to support analysis, reflection, and research.	Making Connections Sections 1, 3–4
CCSS.ELA-Literacy.CCRA.L.1—Demonstrate command of the conventions of standard English grammar and usage when writing or speaking.	Entire Unit
CCSS.ELA-Literacy.CCRA.L.2—Demonstrate command of the conventions of standard English capitalization, punctuation, and spelling when writing.	Entire Unit
CCSS.ELA-Literacy.CCRA.L.4—Determine or clarify the meaning of unknown and multiple-meaning words and phrases by using context clues, analyzing meaningful word parts, and consulting general and specialized reference materials, as appropriate.	Vocabulary Sections 1–5
CCSS.ELA-Literacy.CCRA.L.5—Demonstrate understanding of figurative language, word relationships, and nuances in word meanings.	Making Connections Section 2
CCSS.ELA-Literacy.CCRA.L.6—Acquire and use accurately a range of general academic and domain-specific words and phrases sufficient for reading, writing, speaking, and listening at the college and career readiness level; demonstrate independence in gathering vocabulary knowledge when encountering an unknown term important to comprehension or expression.	Vocabulary Sections 1–5

TESOL and WIDA Standards

The lessons in this book promote English language development for English language learners. The following TESOL and WIDA English Language Development Standards are addressed through the activities in this book:

- **Standard 1:** English language learners communicate for social and instructional purposes within the school setting.
- **Standard 2:** English language learners communicate information, ideas and concepts necessary for academic success in the content area of language arts.

About the Author—Harper Lee

Harper Lee, the award-winning author of *To Kill a Mockingbird*, has become an almost mythical character in America's literary history due to the success of her debut novel and her disappearance from the literary world after its publication.

Born Nelle Harper Lee on April 28, 1926, in Monroeville, Alabama, Lee's childhood was quite similar to the one she wrote for narrator Scout in the novel. Like Scout, Lee grew up in a small southern town during the Great Depression. She was largely raised by her father, a lawyer; her mother was mentally ill and rarely left the house. Lee was a tomboy and close friends with a neighbor boy named Truman Capote, who was the inspiration for the character Dill Harris. Their friendship lasted through adulthood, and Capote also became a successful writer.

Lee attended the University of Alabama to study law, and she spent a year at Oxford University in England as an exchange student. But she began to feel that writing, not law, was her true calling, so she quit school to move to New York and write. In the late 1950s, Lee spent over two years revising and rewriting what would become *To Kill a Mockingbird*. When finally published in 1960, the novel was a huge success, and Lee found herself unexpectedly in the spotlight.

The novel won the Pulitzer Prize in 1961 and was turned into an Academy Award® winning film starring Gregory Peck in 1962. A private person, Lee was overwhelmed by the sudden publicity, demand for interviews, and life in the public eye. Though she wrote a few published essays in 1961 and was rumored to be working on a second book in the late 1960s, *To Kill a Mockingbird* remains Lee's only novel.

Lee withdrew from mainstream society. She accepts awards and honors, but she does not give speeches or interviews. Though some have labeled her a recluse, her friends say she just leads a quiet life. She is active in her church and splits her time between New York and Monroeville, Alabama. Society certainly has not forgotten Lee or her contribution to literature. In 1999, *Library Journal* named *To Kill a Mockingbird* the "best novel of the century," and in 2007, President George W. Bush presented Lee with the Presidential Medal of Freedom.

Check out Harper Lee's website at **http://www.harperlee.com**.

Possible Texts for Text Comparisons

A Tree Grows in Brooklyn by Betty Smith, *The Adventures of Tom Sawyer* by Mark Twain, and *A Time to Kill* by John Grisham could be used for enriching text comparisons. These books deal with similar issues and themes such as race relations, family relationships, and coming-of-age.

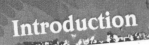

Book Summary of *To Kill a Mockingbird*

An instant classic, millions of people have read *To Kill a Mockingbird* since its publication in 1960. Narrated by an adult Jean Louise Finch (Scout) reflecting on her childhood, the novel addresses timeless issues such as prejudice, social class, gender roles, and family and friend relationships. Set in the fictional town of Maycomb, Alabama, during the Great Depression in the 1930s, the book spans three years and is divided into two parts.

Scout and her older brother, Jem, live with their unconventional father, Atticus, who allows the children to call him by his first name and speaks to them as though they are adults. Atticus, a lawyer and a state legislator, is the moral compass of the story and, as another character states, "is the same in his house as he is on the public streets." Atticus is a widower; Scout's mother passed away when she was two and Jem was six. The Finches also have an African American cook named Calpurnia who is a respected part of their household.

Part one begins with six-year-old Scout, ten-year-old Jem, and their friend and neighbor, Dill Harris, who spends his summers in Maycomb. They spend their days playing outside, making up games, and trying to lure their mysterious neighbor, Boo Radley, out of his house. The children have never seen Boo, but the rumors surrounding him both scare and intrigue the trio. Scout's misadventures at school are also narrated. At one point, she is chastised by her first grade teacher for already knowing how to read and write. She is bored and horribly disappointed with her school experience.

The second part of the book chronicles a trial in which Atticus is defending Tom Robinson, an African American man accused of raping and beating a white woman named Mayella Ewell. Though Mayella and her family are considered disgraceful and the evidence clearly points to Tom's innocence, the biases of the time cause what should be an obvious verdict to become a prejudicial affair. The aftermath of the trial teaches Scout and Jem that it truly is a sin "to kill a mockingbird."

Cross-Curricular Connection

This book could be used during social studies units on the Civil Rights Movement or the Great Depression.

Possible Texts for Text Sets

- Armstrong, William. *Sounder*. HarperCollins, 2002.
- Freedman, Russell. *Children of the Great Depression*. HMH Books for Young People, 2010.
- Levine, Ellen S. *Freedom's Children: Young Civil Rights Activists Tell Their Own Stories*. Puffin, 2000.
- Rawlings, Marjorie Kinnon. *The Yearling*. Scribner, 2002.

Name _____

Date _____

Pre-Reading Theme Thoughts

Directions: Read each of the statements in the first column. Decide if you agree or disagree with the statements. Record your opinion by marking an X in Agree or Disagree for each statement. Explain your choices in the fourth column. There are no right or wrong answers.

Statement	Agree	Disagree	Explain Your Answer
A hero is someone strong and brave who saves the day.			
Rumors about people are usually true.			
In a court of law, a jury will always give a fair and just verdict.			
Anyone can achieve success.			

Vocabulary Overview

Ten key words from this section are provided below with definitions and sentences about how the words are used in the book. Choose one of the vocabulary activity sheets (pages 15 or 16) for students to complete as they read this section. Monitor the students as they work to ensure the definitions they have found are accurate and relate to the text. Finally, discuss these important vocabulary words with the students. If you think these words or other words in the section warrant more time devoted to them, there are suggestions in the introduction for other vocabulary activities (page 5).

Word	Definition	Sentence about Text
taciturn (ch. 1)	not speaking often	Scout's aunt marries a **taciturn** man.
malevolent (ch. 1)	showing a desire to harm another	A **malevolent** phantom lives inside the Radley house.
indigenous (ch. 2)	existing naturally in a particular area	Miss Caroline has the peculiarities **indigenous** to her hometown.
entailment (ch. 2)	restriction of property by limiting its inheritance	Mr. Cunningham speaks with Atticus about his **entailment**.
erratic (ch. 3)	acting in a way that is not regular or expected	Calpurnia's grammar is **erratic** when she is angry.
fractious (ch. 3)	causing trouble	Scout hopes Cal has seen the error of her **fractious** ways.
scuppernongs (ch. 4)	a type of grape native to the southern part of the United States	The children help themselves to others' **scuppernongs**.
benign (ch. 5)	not causing harm	Miss Maudie is a **benign** presence in the neighborhood.
asinine (ch. 5)	stupid or silly	Atticus tells Scout and Jem not to play the **asinine** game.
dismemberment (ch. 6)	to tear apart	Atticus saves Dill from **dismemberment**.

Name _____

Date _____

Understanding Vocabulary Words

Directions: The following words are in this section of the book. Use context clues and reference materials to determine an accurate definition for each word.

Word	Definition
taciturn (ch. 1)	
malevolent (ch. 1)	
indigenous (ch. 2)	
entailment (ch. 2)	
erratic (ch. 3)	
fractious (ch. 3)	
scuppernongs (ch. 4)	
benign (ch. 5)	
asinine (ch. 5)	
dismemberment (ch. 6)	

Name _____

Date _____

During-Reading Vocabulary Activity

Directions: As you read these chapters, record at least eight important words on the lines below. Try to find interesting, difficult, intriguing, special, or funny words. Your words can be long or short. They can be hard or easy to spell. After each word, use context clues in the text and reference materials to define the word.

- _____

- _____

- _____

- _____

- _____

- _____

- _____

- _____

- _____

Directions: Respond to the following questions about the words in this section.

1. Why do Scout and Jem think Boo Radley is **malevolent**?

_____

_____

2. In what ways is Miss Maudie a **benign** presence in the neighborhood?

_____

_____

Analyzing the Literature

Provided below are discussion questions you can use in small groups, with the whole class, or for written assignments. Each question is given at two levels so you can choose the right question for each group of students. Activity sheets with these questions are provided (pages 18–19) if you want students to write their responses. For each question, a few key discussion points are provided for your reference.

Story Element	■ Level 1	▲ Level 2	Key Discussion Points
Setting	Describe the setting of the story.	Why do you think the author chose to set the story in the 1930s instead of in the 1960s when it was written?	The story takes place in the small town of Maycomb, Alabama, during the Great Depression in the 1930s. Everyone knows everyone else and times are tough, with people getting by any way they can. Students' opinions will vary but may include the following ideas: this is when the author grew up, the 1930s show more obvious racism, or people reading the novel in 1960 are able to be more objective about the past instead of the time in which they are living.
Character	Describe Scout and Jem's relationship.	Compare and contrast Scout and Jem's relationship to your relationship with your siblings or other siblings you know.	In many ways, their relationship is typical of siblings. They argue, Scout annoys Jem, and she feels left out when he doesn't include her. However, they are very close and spend a lot of time playing together. They are also protective of each other.
Character	How is Atticus different from others in Maycomb?	What advantages and/or disadvantages could Atticus's differences bring him?	Atticus is educated, as are his children. He doesn't drink, gamble, or hunt like other men in the town and is nonjudgmental. Advantages could be that he is respected and esteemed; disadvantages could be that he might feel disconnected from others because of his differences and has to do the work others do not want to do.
Plot	How has Jem shown bravery in these chapters so far?	Has Jem shown true bravery in his antics with the Radleys? Explain your thinking.	Jem has several situations in which he feels he has shown bravery regarding the Radleys: he touches the house and peeks in the window, helps Scout and Dill escape, and returns for his pants. Students' responses on if these antics show true bravery will vary.

Name _____

Date _____

Analyzing the Literature

Directions: Think about the section you have just read. Read each question and state your response with textual evidence.

1. Describe the setting of the story.

_____

_____

_____

_____

2. Describe Scout and Jem's relationship.

_____

_____

_____

_____

3. How is Atticus different from others in Maycomb?

_____

_____

_____

_____

4. How has Jem shown bravery in these chapters so far?

_____

_____

_____

_____

Name _____

Date _____

▲ Analyzing the Literature

Directions: Think about the section you have just read. Read each question and state your response with textual evidence.

1. Why do you think the author chose to set the story in the 1930s instead of in the 1960s when it was written?

    _____

    _____

    _____

    _____

2. Compare and contrast Scout and Jem's relationship to your relationship with your siblings or other siblings you know.

    _____

    _____

    _____

    _____

3. What advantages and/or disadvantages could Atticus's differences bring him?

    _____

    _____

    _____

    _____

4. Has Jem shown true bravery in his antics with the Radleys? Explain your thinking.

    _____

    _____

    _____

Name _____

Date _____

Reader Response

Directions: Choose one of the following prompts about this section to answer. Be sure you include a topic sentence in your response, use textual evidence to support your opinion, and provide a strong conclusion that summarizes your opinion.

Writing Prompts

- **Narrative Piece**—Scout's teacher, Miss Caroline, is an outsider to Maycomb. When have you felt uncomfortable or like you didn't belong somewhere? Describe the situation and how you handled it.

- **Argument Piece**—Is it wrong for Scout, Jem, and Dill to play their Boo Radley game? Include at least three reasons to support your opinion.

_____

_____

_____

_____

_____

_____

_____

_____

_____

_____

_____

_____

_____

_____

_____

_____

Name _____

Date _____

Close Reading the Literature

Directions: Closely reread the section in chapter 3 in which Walter goes home with Scout and Jem for lunch. Start when they arrive at the house, "By the time we reached our front steps . . . ." Continue reading until Burris leaves the classroom, "He waited until he was sure she was crying." Read each question and then revisit the text to find the evidence that supports your answer.

1. Use the text to describe the different ways Calpurnia and Scout feel about Walter eating at the house.

   _____

   _____

   _____

   _____

2. Though both Walter Cunningham and Burris Ewell are poor, use information in the book to explain how they are different.

   _____

   _____

   _____

   _____

3. Give evidence to show that Miss Caroline is an outsider in Maycomb.

   _____

   _____

   _____

4. According to the section, why is Burris at school?

   _____

   _____

   _____

Name _____

Date _____

Making Connections–The Great Depression

Directions: Understanding the Great Depression is an important part of understanding the novel *To Kill a Mockingbird*. Using resource books, an online encyclopedia, or other websites, do some brief research on this time in American history.

1. When and why did the Great Depression begin?

_____

_____

_____

_____

2. When and how did the Great Depression finally end?

_____

_____

_____

_____

3. Give an example of something the government did to try and help people.

_____

_____

_____

_____

4. Describe at least two other interesting or new things that you learned about the Great Depression.

_____

_____

_____

_____

Name _____

Date _____

Creating with the Story Elements

Directions: Thinking about the story elements of character, setting, and plot in a novel is very important to understanding what is happening and why. Complete **one** of the following activities about what you've read so far. Be creative and have fun!

Characters

Use your imagination and your knowledge of the characters to rewrite the following scene from Dill's point of view. Rewrite the end of chapter 1 when Dill dares Jem to approach the Radley house, argues about lighting a match under a turtle, and runs away after Jem finally touches the house.

Setting

Draw a map of Scout's neighborhood. Use the book to figure out where Scout's neighbors would be located, as well as the school, post office, and any other places mentioned.

Plot

Create a comic strip retelling Scout, Jem, and Dill's escapade in chapter 6 when they attempt to peek in the window at Boo Radley's house.

Vocabulary Overview

Ten key words from this section are provided below with definitions and sentences about how the words are used in the book. Choose one of the vocabulary activity sheets (pages 25 or 26) for students to complete as they read this section. Monitor the students as they work to ensure the definitions they have found are accurate and relate to the text. Finally, discuss these important vocabulary words with the students. If you think these words or other words in the section warrant more time devoted to them, there are suggestions in the introduction for other vocabulary activities (page 5).

Word	Definition	Sentence about Text
ascertaining (ch. 7)	learning something	Jem does not feel the necessity of **ascertaining** the time every five minutes.
aberrations (ch. 8)	unexpected problems	Jem and Scout are blamed for contributing to the **aberrations** of nature.
touchous (ch. 8)	overly sensitive	Atticus is still **touchous** about Jem and Scout playing their Boo Radley game.
accosted (ch. 8)	approached someone and spoke in an angry way	When Scout is on the sidewalk, she is **accosted** by Mr. Avery.
innate (ch. 9)	existing naturally	Scout thinks there is an **innate** attractiveness to curse words.
invective (ch. 9)	rude language	Scout's use of **invective** leaves nothing to the imagination.
rudiments (ch. 10)	basic skills	Uncle Jack instructs Scout and Jem in the **rudiments** of their air rifles.
philippic (ch. 11)	a bitter, verbal attack	Mrs. Dubose yells a **philippic** on the Finch family's moral degeneration.
umbrage (ch. 11)	to feel offended at what someone has said or done	Scout takes **umbrage** at what Mrs. Dubose says about her family's mental hygiene.
rectitude (ch. 11)	being honest and morally correct	Jem tries to enter into a phase of **rectitude** just like Atticus.

Name _____

Date _____

Understanding Vocabulary Words

Directions: The following words are in this section of the book. Use context clues and reference materials to determine an accurate definition for each word.

Word	Definition
ascertaining (ch. 7)	
aberrations (ch. 8)	
touchous (ch. 8)	
accosted (ch. 8)	
innate (ch. 9)	
invective (ch. 9)	
rudiments (ch. 10)	
philippic (ch. 11)	
umbrage (ch. 11)	
rectitude (ch. 11)	

Name _____

Date _____

During-Reading Vocabulary Activity

Directions: As you read these chapters, record at least eight important words on the lines below. Try to find interesting, difficult, intriguing, special, or funny words. Your words can be long or short. They can be hard or easy to spell. After each word, use context clues in the text and reference materials to define the word.

- _____

- _____

- _____

- _____

- _____

- _____

- _____

- _____

- _____

Directions: Respond to the following questions about the words in this section.

1. Why are Jem and Scout **accosted** by Mr. Avery?

_____

_____

2. Why does Uncle Jack instruct Scout and Jem on the **rudiments** of their air rifles instead of Atticus?

_____

_____

Analyzing the Literature

Provided below are discussion questions you can use in small groups, with the whole class, or for written assignments. Each question is given at two levels so you can choose the right question for each group of students. Activity sheets with these questions are provided (pages 28–29) if you want students to write their responses. For each question, a few key discussion points are provided for your reference.

Story Element	■ Level 1	▲ Level 2	Key Discussion Points
Plot	What happens to the tree in which Scout and Jem find the treasured items?	How do Scout's and Jem's reactions differ when they see what happens to the tree?	Mr. Nathan, Boo's brother and caretaker, fills the knothole with cement and tells the children he did it because the tree is dying. Scout seems a bit indifferent. She is disappointed, but Jem is truly upset. He consoles Scout and tells her not to cry, but he is the one who ends up crying about it. He asks Mr. Nathan why he filled the hole and asks Atticus his opinion about the tree's health.
Plot	Why is it a sin to kill a mockingbird?	How do you think the idea of killing a mockingbird can apply to people?	Atticus and Miss Maudie both tell Scout and Jem that mockingbirds do not do anything to bother or annoy people, so they should not be shot. Students' responses will vary, but encourage discussion about harmless people who leave others alone, but are sometimes "hunted" like mockingbirds.
Character	Why do Scout and Jem sometimes feel disappointed or embarrassed about Atticus?	How does the incident with the mad dog change the children's opinions of their father?	Atticus is older than the other fathers and won't play tackle football like they will. The children think he is boring and can't do much other than read. When Atticus shoots the mad dog and they learn he was called "One-Shot Finch" as a younger man, they are impressed. Jem seems to understand Atticus's reasons for not hunting and even states he is a gentleman, just like Atticus.
Plot	Why does Attius say he would have made Jem read to Mrs. Dubose anyway?	How does Mrs. Dubose show true courage?	Atticus knows Mrs. Dubose is dying and trying to overcome her morphine addiction, and he feels Jem reading to Mrs. Dubose will be helpful. Call students' attention to Atticus's quote at the end of chapter 11, "I wanted you to see what real courage is . . . ."

Name _____

Date _____

Analyzing the Literature

Directions: Think about the section you have just read. Read each question and state your response with textual evidence.

1. What happens to the tree in which Scout and Jem find the treasured items?

_____

_____

_____

_____

2. Why is it a sin to kill a mockingbird?

_____

_____

_____

_____

3. Why do Scout and Jem sometimes feel disappointed or embarrassed about Atticus?

_____

_____

_____

_____

4. Why does Attius say he would have made Jem read to Mrs. Dubose anyway?

_____

_____

_____

_____

Name _____

Date _____

▲ Analyzing the Literature

Directions: Think about the section you have just read. Read each question and state your response with textual evidence.

1. How do Scout's and Jem's reactions differ when they see what happens to the tree?

_____

_____

_____

2. How do you think the idea of killing a mockingbird can apply to people?

_____

_____

_____

3. How does the incident with the mad dog change the children's opinions of their father?

_____

_____

_____

4. How does Mrs. Dubose show true courage?

_____

_____

_____

Name _____

Date _____

Reader Response

Directions: Choose one of the following prompts about this section to answer. Be sure you include a topic sentence in your response, use textual evidence to support your opinion, and provide a strong conclusion that summarizes your opinion.

Writing Prompts

- **Argument Piece**—Scout has a hard time getting along with her cousin, Francis, at Christmas. Defend or refute this statement: *Family relationships are among the most difficult relationships in life.*
- **Informative/Explanatory Piece**—In the scene when Atticus shoots the mad dog, what is revealed about his character?

_____

_____

_____

_____

_____

_____

_____

_____

_____

_____

_____

_____

_____

_____

_____

Name _____

Date _____

Close Reading the Literature

Directions: Closely reread the section in chapter 9 when Atticus and Scout discuss the Tom Robinson case. Begin when Scout says, "If you shouldn't be defendin' him . . . ." Continue reading until their conversation ends, "Then Christmas came and disaster struck." Read each question and then revisit the text to find the evidence that supports your answer.

1. According to the text, why does Atticus feel he must defend Tom Robinson?

   _____

   _____

   _____

2. Explain what Atticus means when he says, "Simply because we were licked a hundred years before we started is no reason for us not to try to win."

   _____

   _____

   _____

3. According to Atticus, how will this trial be different from Cousin Ike Finch's recollections from the Civil War?

   _____

   _____

   _____

4. Use the book to explain why Scout walks away from the fight with Cecil Jacobs.

   _____

   _____

   _____

   _____

Name _____

Date _____

Making Connections–Idioms

Directions: The historical setting of this novel gives it a language full of idioms that might be unfamiliar. An idiom is an expression that cannot be understood by the individual words, but instead it has a meaning of its own. Use the text or an idiom dictionary to explain what each word or phrase from the novel means.

1. Scout doesn't believe in **hoodooing**.

   _____

2. Jem **walks on eggs** when he has his grandfather's pocket watch.

   _____

3. Jem says, "**Hidy do**" to Mr. Nathan.

   _____

4. Atticus tells Scout, "**Don't let them get your goat**."

   _____

5. Scout **drew a bead** on Cecil, but drops her fists and doesn't fight.

   _____

6. Atticus says being nearly blind in his left eye is a **tribal curse** of the Finches.

   _____

7. If Atticus has his **druthers**, he will choose a shotgun.

   _____

8. Atticus is a **dead shot** in Maycomb County.

   _____

9. Scout feels Aunt Alexandra **sets her teeth permanently on edge**.

   _____

10. Scout **waits on tenterhooks** to see if Uncle Jack tells Atticus.

    _____

Name _____

Date _____

Creating with the Story Elements

Directions: Thinking about the story elements of character, setting, and plot in a novel is very important to understanding what is happening and why. Complete **one** of the following activities about what you've read so far. Be creative and have fun!

Characters

Create a "Wanted" poster for One-Shot Finch using details and information from the book.

Setting

Though Miss Maudie's house burns to the ground, she does not seem too upset about it. Using comments Miss Maudie shares about her hobbies and interests, draw a new house and yard for her.

Plot

Imagine Jem is attending Mrs. Dubose's funeral and is asked to give a brief eulogy. Write a paragraph from Jem's point-of-view that describes his relationship with Mrs. Dubose and what he learned from her.

Vocabulary Overview

Ten key words from this section are provided below with definitions and sentences about how the words are used in the book. Choose one of the vocabulary activity sheets (pages 35 or 36) for students to complete as they read this section. Monitor the students as they work to ensure the definitions they have found are accurate and relate to the text. Finally, discuss these important vocabulary words with the students. If you think these words or other words in the section warrant more time devoted to them, there are suggestions in the introduction for other vocabulary activities (page 5).

Word	Definition	Sentence about Text
altercation (ch. 12)	a noisy argument	After an **altercation**, Jem tells Scout she should start acting like a girl.
contemptuously (ch. 12)	showing strong dislike or disapproval	Calpurnia speaks quietly and **contemptuously** to Lula.
prerogative (ch. 13)	a right or privilege	Aunt Alexandra exercises her **prerogative** to do what she wants.
edification (ch. 14)	improving a person's mind or character	Jem gives Scout things to read for her **edification** and instruction.
fortitude (ch. 14)	mental strength or courage	Dill waits with **fortitude** during his Aunt Rachel's lecture.
venerable (ch. 15)	old and respected	The Maycomb jail is the most **venerable** and hideous building in the county.
acquiescence (ch. 15)	to agree to something by staying silent and not arguing	Scout is used to prompt, if not always cheerful, **acquiescence** to Atticus's instructions.
profane (ch. 16)	showing disrespect for something religious	Mr. Underwood is an intense, **profane** little man.
acrimonious (ch. 17)	angry and bitter	Scout can tell when a debate becomes more **acrimonious** than professional.
tenet (ch. 17)	an idea important to a group	Never ask a question you don't know the answer to is a **tenet** Scout learns as a child.

Understanding Vocabulary Words

Directions: The following words are in this section of the book. Use context clues and reference materials to determine an accurate definition for each word.

Word	Definition
altercation (ch. 12)	
contemptuously (ch. 12)	
prerogative (ch. 13)	
edification (ch. 14)	
fortitude (ch. 14)	
venerable (ch. 15)	
acquiescence (ch. 15)	
profane (ch. 16)	
acrimonious (ch. 17)	
tenet (ch. 17)	

Name _____

Date _____

During-Reading Vocabulary Activity

Directions: As you read these chapters, record at least eight important words on the lines below. Try to find interesting, difficult, intriguing, special, or funny words. Your words can be long or short. They can be hard or easy to spell. After each word, use context clues in the text and reference materials to define the word.

- _____
- _____
- _____
- _____
- _____
- _____
- _____
- _____
- _____
- _____

Directions: Now, organize your words. Rewrite each of your words on a sticky note. Work as a group to create a bar graph of your words. You should stack any words that are the same on top of one another. Different words appear in different columns. Finally, discuss with a group why certain words were chosen more often than other words.

Analyzing the Literature

Provided below are discussion questions you can use in small groups, with the whole class, or for written assignments. Each question is given at two levels so you can choose the right question for each group of students. Activity sheets with these questions are provided (pages 38–39) if you want students to write their responses. For each question, a few key discussion points are provided for your reference.

Story Element	■ Level 1	▲ Level 2	Key Discussion Points
Character	What does Scout notice about Calpurnia's way of speaking at church?	What reason does Calpurnia give for speaking differently at her church?	Scout notices Calpurnia speaking in the dialect of the other African Americans at church. Cal explains to Scout that she talks that way because it would be out of place for her to speak like "white-folks" and the other African Americans would think she was showing off.
Setting	How does Aunt Alexandra fit into Maycomb society?	How does Aunt Alexandra's idea of proper Finch behavior in Maycomb affect Atticus?	Aunt Alexandra is welcomed by the others in town and quickly joins clubs and social circles. She is appalled that Atticus has not taught the children about their fine heritage. Atticus attempts to talk to the children about it, but Scout and Jem are so confused and hurt, he quickly retracts his speech and tells them to forget about it.
Character	When Dill returns, what does Jem do that Scout feels breaks their code of childhood?	When Jem tells Atticus about Dill's return, what do we learn about Jem's character?	Jem tells Atticus that Dill has run away and is in the house. This reaction shows Jem's maturity and his willingness to do what he feels is right even if it makes others close to him unhappy (a trait Atticus has as well).
Character	Briefly describe Bob Ewell's testimony at the trial.	Why does Bob Ewell receive warnings from the judge, yet endear himself to the audience in the courtroom?	Mr. Ewell bluntly states that as he was returning from chopping wood, he heard his daughter screaming. When he approached the house, he saw Tom Robinson raping his daughter. Mr. Ewell says Mayella was beaten up and the room was a mess. He receives warnings from the judge for his lack of tact and being disrespectful when answering questions. The audience finds humor in his sarcastic and indelicate responses.

Name _____

Date _____

Analyzing the Literature

Directions: Think about the section you have just read. Read each question and state your response with textual evidence.

1. What does Scout notice about Calpurnia's way of speaking at church?

_____

_____

_____

_____

2. How does Aunt Alexandra fit into Maycomb society?

_____

_____

_____

_____

3. When Dill returns, what does Jem do that Scout feels breaks their code of childhood?

_____

_____

_____

_____

4. Briefly describe Bob Ewell's testimony at the trial.

_____

_____

_____

_____

▲ Analyzing the Literature

Directions: Think about the section you have just read. Read each question and state your response with textual evidence.

1. What reason does Calpurnia give for speaking differently at her church?

   _____

   _____

   _____

2. How does Aunt Alexandra's idea of proper Finch behavior in Maycomb affect Atticus?

   _____

   _____

   _____

3. When Jem tells Atticus about Dill's return, what do we learn about Jem's character?

   _____

   _____

   _____

4. Why does Bob Ewell receive warnings from the judge, yet endear himself to the audience in the courtroom?

   _____

   _____

   _____

Name _____

Date _____

Reader Response

Directions: Choose one of the following prompts about this section to answer. Be sure you include a topic sentence in your response, use textual evidence to support your opinion, and provide a strong conclusion that summarizes your opinion.

Writing Prompts

- **Narrative Piece**—Calpurnia's church is raising money to help Tom Robinson's family. Describe ways that you have worked together with friends or family to help others.
- **Argument Piece**—Why do you think Atticus does not tell Scout and Jem he was appointed to defend Tom Robinson? Defend your opinion with details about Atticus's personality.

_____

_____

_____

_____

_____

_____

_____

_____

_____

_____

_____

_____

_____

_____

_____

Name _____

Date _____

Close Reading the Literature

Directions: Closely reread the section at the end of chapter 15 when Scout approaches the mob. Continue until the beginning of chapter 16 when Scout, Jem, and Atticus are discussing the previous night, "That was enough." Read each question and then revisit the text to find the evidence that supports your answer.

1. Use the text to describe Atticus and Jem's interaction when Atticus realizes the children are in danger.

   _____

   _____

   _____

   _____

2. Is Atticus upset with Jem when he refuses to obey? Use text evidence in your response.

   _____

   _____

   _____

3. According to the section, why does Atticus feel he can speak freely in front of Calpurnia?

   _____

   _____

   _____

4. Use Atticus's response at breakfast to explain how Scout helped him avoid being hurt by the mob.

   _____

   _____

   _____

   _____

Name _____

Date _____

Making Connections–Carving Soap

Two of the treasures Scout and Jem find in the knothole are soap carvings of a boy and girl resembling themselves. Try a soap carving of your own!

Materials

- bar of soap (1 per student)
- newspaper
- plastic knife
- toothpick
- pen
- water

Procedure

1. Lay the newspaper down to protect your work surface.
2. Decide what you will carve and draw it on the soap with the pen. Fish, flowers, trees, hearts, boats, and turtles are good shapes for beginners.
3. Carefully use the plastic knife to cut away the area outside the pen outline. Remove only small areas at a time to avoid accidentally cutting off a large piece.
4. Add details and designs to your carving with the toothpick.
5. Rub a small amount of water over the finished design with your finger to smooth the surface.
6. Allow the soap to cure for 24 hours.

Response

1. For what reasons was Scout afraid of the figures at first?

   _____

   _____

   _____

   _____

2. Why do you think the figures were placed in the knothole?

   _____

   _____

   _____

   _____

   _____

Creating with the Story Elements

Directions: Thinking about the story elements of character, setting, and plot in a novel is very important to understanding what is happening and why. Complete **one** of the following activities about what you've read so far. Be creative and have fun!

Characters

Miss Maudie and Aunt Alexandra are both influential women in Scout's life. Make a Venn diagram comparing and contrasting the two women.

Setting

Use details from the book to draw a bird's-eye view of the courtroom scene. Include the areas for the judge, lawyers, jury, and all spectators.

Plot

Use the testimonies of Sheriff Tate and Mr. Ewell to create a flow chart of the order of events said to have happened on the evening that Tom Robinson is accused of raping Mayella. The flow chart should have 5–7 events.

Vocabulary Overview

Ten key words from this section are provided below with definitions and sentences about how the words are used in the book. Choose one of the vocabulary activity sheets (pages 45 or 46) for students to complete as they read this section. Monitor the students as they work to ensure the definitions they have found are accurate and relate to the text. Finally, discuss these important vocabulary words with the students. If you think these words or other words in the section warrant more time devoted to them, there are suggestions in the introduction for other vocabulary activities (page 5).

Word	Definition	Sentence about Text
mollified (ch. 18)	calmed down	**Mollified**, Mayella gives Atticus a terrified glance and continues talking.
expunge (ch. 19)	to remove completely	Judge Taylor tells the court reporter to **expunge** the outburst in the court records.
corroborative (ch. 20)	to help prove something by providing evidence	Atticus says there is an absence of **corroborative** evidence.
temerity (ch. 20)	to be confident in a way that seems rude or shocking	Tom Robinson has the **temerity** to feel sorry for a white woman.
demurred (ch. 21)	disagreed politely	Reverend Sykes **demurs** to Jem that the trial is not appropriate for Scout to hear.
impassive (ch. 22)	not showing emotion	Atticus is standing on the corner as his **impassive** self again.
furtive (ch. 23)	done in a secret way to avoid being noticed	Aunt Alexandra worries that the Ewells will do something **furtive**.
sordid (ch. 23)	very bad or dirty	The frail ladies need to be protected from **sordid** cases.
duress (ch. 24)	threats meant to make someone do something	Under **duress**, the man sees nothing wrong with singing.
brevity (ch. 24)	using few words to say something	When Miss Maudie is angry, her **brevity** is icy.

Name _____

Date _____

Understanding Vocabulary Words

Directions: The following words are in this section of the book. Use context clues and reference materials to determine an accurate definition for each word.

Word	Definition
mollified (ch. 18)	
expunge (ch. 19)	
corroborative (ch. 20)	
temerity (ch. 20)	
demurred (ch. 21)	
impassive (ch. 22)	
furtive (ch. 23)	
sordid (ch. 23)	
duress (ch. 24)	
brevity (ch. 24)	

Name _____

Date _____

During-Reading Vocabulary Activity

Directions: As you read these chapters, record at least eight important words on the lines below. Try to find interesting, difficult, intriguing, special, or funny words. Your words can be long or short. They can be hard or easy to spell. After each word, use context clues in the text and reference materials to define the word.

- _____
- _____
- _____
- _____
- _____
- _____
- _____
- _____
- _____
- _____

Directions: Respond to the following questions about the words in this section.

1. What makes Mayella feel **mollified** before Atticus questions her?

_____

_____

2. Why is the fact that Tom has the **temerity** to feel sorry for Mayella such a problem for the jury?

_____

_____

Analyzing the Literature

Provided below are discussion questions you can use in small groups, with the whole class, or for written assignments. Each question is given at two levels so you can choose the right question for each group of students. Activity sheets with these questions are provided (pages 48–49) if you want students to write their responses. For each question, a few key discussion points are provided for your reference.

Story Element	■ Level 1	▲ Level 2	Key Discussion Points
Plot	What flaw does Atticus uncover in Mayella's testimony about Tom Robinson beating her?	What is Mayella's reaction when she realizes Atticus has found a flaw in her retelling of the events?	Mayella says the right side of her face was bruised and beaten. This would logically mean a left-handed person hit her. Her father is left handed, but Tom Robinson's left hand is disfigured and unusable. When she realizes this, she changes her story and says she ducked and the punch glanced off.
Character	Why is Dill so upset during Tom's cross-examination?	How does Dill's reaction to Tom's cross-examination show his true character?	Dill begins crying and is taken from the courtroom by Scout. He is upset because he feels Mr. Gilmer, the prosecuting attorney, is being rude to Tom and treating him badly during his questioning. Dill has a child's innocence and seems to have little prejudice. Dill believes that no one should be spoken to or treated that way. Race does not matter to Dill, and he serves as the novel's conscience. (Also, remember the children's conversation earlier in the novel about lighting a match under a turtle and Dill's defense of the turtle.)
Setting	From where are the majority of the jurors?	Why are the townspeople not usually on juries?	Most of the jurors are from the farming community outside of the town; Jem refers to them as "out in the woods." Atticus says the townspeople do not want to be on the juries. They do not want to take sides in matters that might affect their businesses, so they get out of jury duty.
Character	What happens to Tom in prison?	Why is Tom's death especially upsetting to Atticus?	In prison, Tom loses hope and does not believe in his chances at an appeal. He tries to escape by climbing the fence and is shot and killed. Atticus is upset about his death and its impact on Tom's family, but also because he was very optimistic about Tom's chances for an appeal and acquittal.

Name _____

Date _____

■ Analyzing the Literature

Directions: Think about the section you have just read. Read each question and state your response with textual evidence.

1. What flaw does Atticus uncover in Mayella's testimony about Tom Robinson beating her?

_____

_____

_____

_____

2. Why is Dill so upset during Tom's cross-examination?

_____

_____

_____

_____

3. From where are the majority of the jurors?

_____

_____

_____

_____

4. What happens to Tom in prison?

_____

_____

_____

_____

Name _____

Date _____

▲ Analyzing the Literature

Directions: Think about the section you have just read. Read each question and state your response with textual evidence.

1. What is Mayella's reaction when she realizes Atticus has found a flaw in her retelling of the events?

_____

_____

_____

2. How does Dill's reaction to Tom's cross-examination show his true character?

_____

_____

_____

3. Why are the townspeople not usually on juries?

_____

_____

_____

4. Why was Tom's death especially upsetting to Atticus?

_____

_____

_____

Name

Date

Reader Response

Directions: Choose one of the following prompts about this section to answer. Be sure you include a topic sentence in your response, use textual evidence to support your opinion, and provide a strong conclusion that summarizes your opinion.

Writing Prompts

- **Argument Piece**—Jem says there are four kinds of folks, but Scout thinks there is just one kind. With whom do you agree? Give examples to support your opinion.
- **Informative/Explanatory Piece**—Bob Ewell threatens everyone involved with the trial. What do you think he might do? Choose at least two people and explain your prediction.

Name _____

Date _____

Close Reading the Literature

Directions: Closely reread the section in chapter 20 when Atticus is giving his closing argument. Begin with, "'Gentlemen,' he was saying, 'I shall be brief . . . .'" Read until Atticus finishes, "In the name of God, do your duty." Read each question and then revisit the text to find the evidence that supports your answer.

1. Use the text to explain the lack of evidence in the trial.

_____

_____

_____

_____

2. According to this section, why does Mayella lie about what happened?

_____

_____

_____

_____

3. Based on this scene, why do the Ewells feel their testimony will not be doubted?

_____

_____

_____

_____

4. Explain why "All men are created equal" is both true and false.

_____

_____

_____

_____

Name _____

Date _____

Making Connections–Gender Roles

Directions: The contrast between Aunt Alexandra and Miss Maudie adds a small focus on gender roles to the novel. Though still present in modern-day society, during the 1930s the lines were firm on what was and was not acceptable for females. Use examples from the book, prior knowledge, or outside resources to complete the table with expectations for women.

	Expectations for Women in the 1930s	Expectations for Women Today
clothing		
hobbies and interests		
chores		
careers		

1. Do you feel there are still gender role prejudices today? Explain.

   _____

   _____

   _____

2. Describe any instances when gender roles are appropriate.

   _____

   _____

   _____

Name _____

Date _____

Creating with the Story Elements

Directions: Thinking about the story elements of character, setting, and plot in a novel is very important to understanding what is happening and why. Complete **one** of the following activities about what you've read so far. Be creative and have fun!

Characters

Make a list of at least 10 characters in *To Kill a Mockingbird* and write how Tom Robinson's guilty verdict affects each. Include both main and secondary characters.

Setting

Based on information in the book, draw the Ewells' house and the surrounding area. Clearly label the different locations on your map.

Plot

Imagine you are a reporter at Mr. Underwood's newspaper, *The Maycomb Tribune*. Write a news article covering the events of the trial. Be sure to include a headline and quotations from the witnesses and lawyers.

Vocabulary Overview

Ten key words from this section are provided below with definitions and sentences about how the words are used in the book. Choose one of the vocabulary activity sheets (pages 55 or 56) for students to complete as they read this section. Monitor the students as they work to ensure the definitions they have found are accurate and relate to the text. Finally, discuss these important vocabulary words with the students. If you think these words or other words in the section warrant more time devoted to them, there are suggestions in the introduction for other vocabulary activities (page 5).

Word	Definition	Sentence about Text
demise (ch. 25)	a person's death	The town gossips share their views on Tom Robinson's **demise**.
spurious (ch. 26)	untrue or based on bad reasoning	Miss Gates thinks *The Grit Paper* is a **spurious** publication.
annals (ch. 27)	historical records	Mr. Ewell makes himself unique in the **annals** of the 1930s.
florid (ch. 27)	too fancy or complicated	While lost in the **florid** writing, Judge Taylor hears a noise.
purloined (ch. 27)	stole	Miss Tutti is sure the traveling fur sellers **purloined** her furniture.
ascertain (ch. 28)	to find out something for sure	The explorers look at a tree to **ascertain** which way is south.
pinioned (ch. 28)	tied up or held a person's arms or legs	Scout runs into her attacker with her arms tightly **pinioned**.
reprimand (ch. 29)	to speak in a critical way	Scout puts her arm down so Atticus won't **reprimand** her for pointing.
stolidly (ch. 30)	showing no emotion	Mr. Tate **stolidly** says that Mr. Ewell fell on his knife.
raling (ch. 31)	painful	Boo Radley has a deep, **raling** cough.

Name _____

Date _____

Understanding Vocabulary Words

Directions: The following words are in this section of the book. Use context clues and reference materials to determine an accurate definition for each word.

Word	Definition
demise (ch. 25)	
spurious (ch. 26)	
annals (ch. 27)	
florid (ch. 27)	
purloined (ch. 27)	
ascertain (ch. 28)	
pinioned (ch. 28)	
reprimand (ch. 29)	
stolidly (ch. 30)	
raling (ch. 31)	

Name _____

Date _____

During-Reading Vocabulary Activity

Directions: As you read these chapters, choose five important words from the story. Use these words to complete the word flow chart below. On each arrow, write a word. In each box, explain how the connected pair of words relates to each other. An example for the words *annals* and *florid* has been done for you.

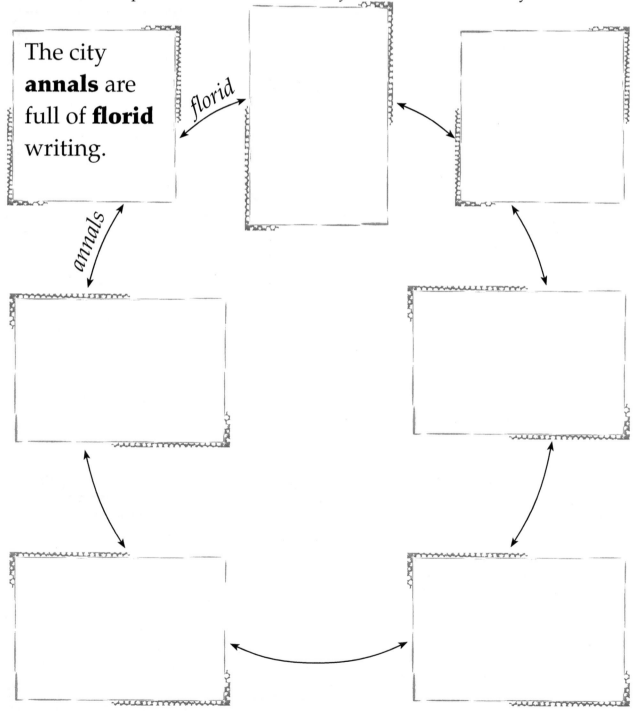

The city **annals** are full of **florid** writing.

florid

annals

Analyzing the Literature

Provided below are discussion questions you can use in small groups, with the whole class, or for written assignments. Each question is given at two levels so you can choose the right question for each group of students. Activity sheets with these questions are provided (pages 58–59) if you want students to write their responses. For each question, a few key discussion points are provided for your reference.

Story Element	■ Level 1	▲ Level 2	Key Discussion Points
Plot	What does Mr. Underwood write about in his newspaper editorial?	Explain what is meant when Scout realizes, "Tom was a dead man the minute Mayella Ewell opened her mouth and screamed."	Mr. Underwood writes about Tom Robinson's death. In simple language, he writes that he thinks it is a sin to "kill cripples" and compares Tom's death to the innocent killing of songbirds. When reading the editorial, Scout finally realizes that no matter what the evidence stated, Tom was going to be convicted simply because a white woman had accused him of a crime and he is an African American.
Character	Describe Scout's imagined conversation with Boo Radley.	How does Scout's fantasy about her conversation with Boo show she is maturing?	Scout imagines walking by Boo's house and finding him sitting on the porch. She will greet him cheerfully, he will answer like they chat often, and they will discuss the weather. Scout is showing some maturity because she is no longer scared to pass the house. While she still longs to see him, she wants to meet with him in a respectful, neighborly way instead of the pranks and trespassing ways of the past.
Plot	What really happens to Bob Ewell?	Why is Sheriff Tate so adamant that Bob Ewell fell on his knife?	Boo kills Bob Ewell with a knife from the Radley kitchen. The sheriff knows what really happened, but he understands why Boo did it and feels that letting the townspeople know would be cruel to Boo. It would upset Boo's quiet, solitary life and bring unwanted attention.
Character	Why will Scout lead Boo around her house but not back to his home?	How does Scout's refusal to lead Boo home show her growing acceptance of her femininity?	Scout realizes Boo is a fragile man and politely takes over leading in her house. But she knows on the street, others might see and she does not want to hurt Boo's masculinity in the eyes of the public. Scout understands what is expected of her as a lady, and she obliges in public, while still staying true to herself in her home.

Name _____

Date _____

Analyzing the Literature

Directions: Think about the section you have just read. Read each question and state your response with textual evidence.

1. What does Mr. Underwood write about in his newspaper editorial?

_____

_____

_____

_____

2. Describe Scout's imagined conversation with Boo Radley.

_____

_____

_____

_____

3. What really happens to Bob Ewell?

_____

_____

_____

_____

4. Why will Scout lead Boo around her house but not back to his home?

_____

_____

_____

_____

▲ Analyzing the Literature

Directions: Think about the section you have just read. Read each question and state your response with textual evidence.

1. Explain what is meant when Scout realizes, "Tom was a dead man the minute Mayella Ewell opened her mouth and screamed."

_____

_____

_____

_____

2. How does Scout's fantasy about her conversation with Boo show she is maturing?

_____

_____

_____

_____

3. Why is Sheriff Tate so adamant that Bob Ewell fell on his knife?

_____

_____

_____

_____

4. How does Scout's refusal to lead Boo home show her growing acceptance of her femininity?

_____

_____

_____

Name _____

Date _____

Reader Response

Directions: Choose one of the following prompts about this section to answer. Be sure you include a topic sentence in your response, use textual evidence to support your opinion, and provide a strong conclusion that summarizes your opinion.

Writing Prompts

- **Narrative Piece**—Scout leads Boo around her home, but she allows him to escort her as a proper gentleman outside. Describe a time when you did the proper thing for public appearances, while you acted differently in private.
- **Argument Piece**—Sheriff Tate says Bob Ewell fell on his knife even though Boo actually killed him. Was this the right thing for a sheriff to do? Give at least two reasons to support your opinion.

_____

_____

_____

_____

_____

_____

_____

_____

_____

_____

_____

_____

_____

_____

Name _____

Date _____

Close Reading the Literature

Directions: Closely reread the section in chapter 26 about the current events period. Begin with, "I was forced to one day in school . . . ." Continue reading until the end of the chapter. Read each question and then revisit the text to find the evidence that supports your answer.

1. According to the text, why don't current events work well in Maycomb?

   _____

   _____

   _____

   _____

2. Explain Miss Gates's description of the difference between Germany's and America's governments.

   _____

   _____

   _____

   _____

3. Use this section to explain the hypocrisy Scout discovers about Miss Gates.

   _____

   _____

   _____

   _____

4. According to Atticus, why does Jem have such a strong reaction to the trial?

   _____

   _____

   _____

   _____

Name _____

Date _____

Making Connections—Coming of Age

To Kill a Mockingbird is considered a "coming-of-age novel," meaning the main character grows and changes during the story. Scout experiences maturation, moral growth, and loss of innocence as she tells readers of her childhood.

Directions: Write about an experience that was a "coming-of-age" moment for you. It could be a lesson you learned, an event that deepened your sense of right and wrong, or a time you felt your maturity grow.

Name _____

Date _____

Creating with the Story Elements

Directions: Thinking about the story elements of character, setting, and plot in a novel is very important to understanding what is happening and why. Complete **one** of the following activities about what you've read so far. Be creative and have fun!

Characters

Write a letter to Boo Radley as Scout. Tell Boo all of the things you think Scout would want to share with him.

Setting

Being set in the South in the 1930s is integral to the plot of the novel. Imagine the setting or the time period is different for the novel. Explain the change you made and list at least 10 things that might be different in the novel because of the new setting or year.

Plot

Both Tom Robinson and Boo Radley are considered *mockingbirds* by literary critics. The two characters have many things in common, but they also have significant differences. Create a table with characteristics and information about each man that makes him a literary *mockingbird*.

Name _____

Date _____

Post-Reading Theme Thoughts

Directions: Read each of the statements in the first column. Choose a main character from *To Kill a Mockingbird*. Think about that character's point of view. From that character's perspective, decide if the character would agree or disagree with the statements. Record the character's opinion by marking an X in Agree or Disagree for each statement. Explain your choices in the fourth column using text evidence.

Character I Chose: _____

Statement	Agree	Disagree	Explain Your Answer
A hero is someone strong and brave who saves the day.			
Rumors about people are usually true.			
In a court of law, a jury will always give a fair and just verdict.			
Anyone can achieve success.			

Culminating Activity: Scout's Scrapbook

Overview: *To Kill a Mockingbird* covers almost three years of Scout's life, beginning the summer before she starts school and ending when she is in the third grade. Many scary, exciting, and sad things happen to her during the novel. Narrating the tale as an adult, Scout proves to have an excellent memory of the events that transpired.

Directions: Create a list of 10 important events that occur in the story. These ideas will be used to create a scrapbook of Scout's childhood.

- _____

- _____

- _____

- _____

- _____

- _____

- _____

- _____

- _____

Name _____

Date _____

Culminating Activity: Scout's Scrapbook (cont.)

Directions: When you have completed your list of 10 events from the novel, make a creative and imaginative scrapbook for Scout. You can create your scrapbook on paper or using a computer design program.

Each page in your scrapbook should have the following components:

A picture of an event from the novel

- drawings
- computer-generated images
- images from the movie *To Kill a Mockingbird*.

A description of what is happening in the picture

- **Scout's thoughts, feelings, or opinions about that event**

Name _____

Date _____

Comprehension Assessment

Directions: Circle the letter for the best response to each question.

1. What is the meaning of *mockingbird* as it is used in the book?

   A. a songbird

   B. a helpful person in the community

   C. a poor person

   D. an innocent person

2. Which detail from the book best supports your answer to question 1?

   E. "Atticus is the same in his house as he is on the public streets."

   F. "Mockingbirds don't do one thing but sing their hearts out for us."

   G. "It's not against the law for a citizen to prevent a crime, which is exactly what he [Boo] did."

   H. "The Cunninghams never took anything they can't pay back—no church baskets, and no scrip stamps."

3. What is the main idea of the text below?

   _____

   _____

   _____

   Atticus: "I wanted you to see what real courage is, instead of getting the idea that courage is a man with a gun in his hand. It's when you know you're licked before you begin but you begin anyway and you see it through no matter what. You rarely win, but sometimes you do."

4. Choose **two** details to support your answer to question 3.

   A. Atticus can't win the trial, but he is able to keep the jury deliberating for a long time.

   B. If a white man cheats an African American man, there is something wrong with that white man.

   C. Serving on a jury forces a man to declare himself on something.

   D. Tom Robinson is a guilty man the moment Mayella Ewell opens her mouth and screams.

Comprehension Assessment *(cont.)*

5. Which statement best expresses one of the themes of the book?

    E. People are often blind to their own prejudices.

    F. Rumors are usually true.

    G. Adults know better than children.

    H. Deep down, most people are evil.

6. What detail from the book provides the best evidence for your answer to number 5?

    A. "When they finally saw him, he hadn't done any of those things . . . Atticus, he was real nice . . . "

    B. "Jem, how can you hate Hitler so bad an' then turn around and be ugly about folks right at home . . . ."

    C. To Mr. Raymond, "You mean all you drink in that sack's Coca-Cola?"

    D. "You know [Uncle Jack] told you you'd get in trouble if you used words like that!"

7. What is the purpose of these sentences from the book: "I don't know, but they did it. They've done it before and they did it tonight and they'll do it again and when they do it—seems that only children weep."

    _____

    _____

    _____

    _____

8. Which other quotation from the story serves a similar purpose?

    E. "Things haven't caught up with that one's instinct yet. Let him get a little older and he won't get sick and cry."

    F. "The one thing that doesn't abide by majority rule is a person's conscience."

    G. "You never really understand a person until you consider things from his point of view—until you climb into his skin and walk around in it."

    H. "Come along, Mr. Arthur, you don't know the house real well. I'll just take you to the porch, sir."

Name _____

Date _____

Response to Literature: Civil Rights Court Cases

Overview: *To Kill a Mockingbird* is a fictional work published in 1960. However, events similar to the trial of Tom Robinson during the story's setting of the 1930s are not imagined. In the decades following the Great Depression, African Americans and their supporters began fighting prejudicial laws and unfair treatment. This fight is called the Civil Rights Movement, and many important victories in court cases helped bring equality for African Americans.

Brief summaries of a few pivotal cases are listed below:

- *Shelley v. Kraemer* (1948)—Several white families in a St. Louis neighborhood had a written covenant stating no property could be sold to any African American. The Shelleys, who were African Americans, bought property in the neighborhood.
- *Brown v. Board of Education* (1954)—Under the "separate but equal" rule, African American and white children attended segregated schools. Several individual cases joined together as one large case to fight this injustice.
- *Browder v. Gayle* (1956)—Bus segregation was the norm, with whites up front and African Americans in the back. African Americans were also expected to give up their seats for white people. When Rosa Parks refused to move from her seat, a bus boycott and court case began.

Directions: Select one of these court cases and in an essay compare and contrast it with Tom Robinson's trial. How does the year in which each trial occurred affect its outcome? What might have been different about Tom's trial if it had been set in the author's present-day year of 1960?

Your essay should follow these guidelines:

- Be at least 1,000 words in length.
- Cite information about the historical trial.
- Compare/contrast the trial with the one in the novel.
- Cite at least three references from the novel.
- Provide a conclusion that summarizes your thoughts and findings.

Final essays are due on _____.

Name _____

Date _____

Response to Literature Rubric

Directions: Use this rubric to evaluate student responses.

	Exceptional Writing	Quality Writing	Developing Writing
Focus and Organization	☐ States a clear opinion and elaborates well. Engages the reader from hook through the middle to the conclusion. Demonstrates clear understanding of the intended audience and purpose of the piece.	☐ Provides a clear and consistent opinion. Maintains a clear perspective and supports it through elaborating details. Makes the opinion clear in the opening hook and summarizes well in the conclusion.	☐ Provides an inconsistent point of view. Does not support the topic adequately or misses pertinent information. Provides lack of clarity in the beginning, middle, and conclusion.
Text Evidence	☐ Provides comprehensive and accurate support. Includes relevant and worthwhile text references.	☐ Provides limited support. Provides few supporting text references.	☐ Provides very limited support for the text. Provides no supporting text references.
Written Expression	☐ Uses descriptive and precise language with clarity and intention. Maintains a consistent voice and uses an appropriate tone that supports meaning. Uses multiple sentence types and transitions well between ideas.	☐ Uses a broad vocabulary. Maintains a consistent voice and supports a tone and feelings through language. Varies sentence length and word choices.	☐ Uses a limited and unvaried vocabulary. Provides an inconsistent or weak voice and tone. Provides little to no variation in sentence type and length.
Language Conventions	☐ Capitalizes, punctuates, and spells accurately. Demonstrates complete thoughts within sentences, with accurate subject-verb agreement. Uses paragraphs appropriately and with clear purpose.	☐ Capitalizes, punctuates, and spells accurately. Demonstrates complete thoughts within sentences and appropriate grammar. Paragraphs are properly divided and supported.	☐ Incorrectly capitalizes, punctuates, and spells. Uses fragmented or run-on sentences. Utilizes poor grammar overall. Paragraphs are poorly divided and developed.

The responses provided here are just examples of what the students may answer. Many accurate responses are possible for the questions throughout this unit.

During-Reading Vocabulary Activity—Section 1:
Chapters 1–6 (page 16)

1. Scout and Jem think Boo is **malevolent** because of the rumors. They think Boo wanders the streets at night, peeks in the neighbor's window, and stabs his family with scissors.

2. Miss Maudie is a **benign** presence because she does not judge the children and allows Scout to spend time with her.

Close Reading the Literature—Section 1:
Chapters 1–6 (page 21)

1. Calpurnia feels Walter is a guest and should be treated accordingly, while Scout thinks he's "just a Cunningham." She thinks she should be free to treat him with less respect than another guest.

2. Walter is polite, attends school when he can, and is able to carry on an adult conversation with Atticus. His family is poor, but it has dignity and insists on paying off their debts. Burris is filthy and very disrespectful to Miss Caroline, calling her obscene names and making her cry. His family does nothing to help themselves and tries to take advantage of the system.

3. Miss Caroline is an outsider because she is not familiar with Maycomb's ways. For example, she does not understand what being a Cunningham really means and is not familiar with the Ewell's disgraceful standing in the community. She also reads the children a silly, imaginative book that is not socially fitting a class of poverty-stricken children who work in the fields.

4. Burris is at school as part of his family's compromise with the truant lady. The Ewell children come on the first day to appease her and are then counted absent for the rest of the school year.

Making Connections—Section 1:
Chapters 1–6 (page 22)

1. The Great Depression began on October 29, 1929, when the stock market crashed.

2. It ended in late 1939 when the United States became involved in World War II.

3. The government started many programs through the New Deal to help the citizens. Examples are the Social Security Act, the Public Works Administration, and Works Project Administration.

4. Student responses will vary.

During-Reading Vocabulary Activity—Section 2:
Chapters 7–11 (page 26)

1. Jem and Scout are **accosted** by Mr. Avery because he blames the children for the unusually cold weather and snow.

2. Uncle Jack is teaching them the **rudiments** of their air rifles because Atticus will not. Uncle Jack says Atticus does not care for guns.

Close Reading the Literature—Section 2:
Chapters 7–11 (page 31)

1. Atticus says he must defend Tom Robinson because if he doesn't, he will not be able to keep his self-respect. He does not feel he can represent the town in the legislature or even make Scout and Jem obey him if he does not do what he knows is right.

2. Atticus means that even though events of the past might influence the town's present-day decisions, it is still important to work toward the change that needs to happen. He is not afraid to fight even though he knows he will lose because doing the right thing is more important than winning.

3. The trial will be different from the Civil War because in the Civil War, people were fighting strangers and were often far away from their homes. This trial will take place in Maycomb, among Atticus's neighbors and friends.

4. Scout walks away from Cecil because Atticus asks her to avoid fights. Atticus does not ask her to do many things for him, so she realizes this must be important and wants to honor him.

Making Connections—Section 2:
Chapters 7–11 (page 32)

1. hoodooing—folk magic, like voodoo

2. walks on eggs—to act very carefully

3. hidy do—informal way to say hello

4. don't let them get your goat—do not be discouraged or let others make you angry

5. drew a bead—to aim at something, as if to shoot

6. tribal curse—a problem or illness in a family

7. druthers—a person's choice

8. dead shot—shooting without mistakes

9. sets her teeth permanently on edge—to upset someone

10. waits on tenterhooks—waiting nervously or impatiently

Close Reading the Literature—Section 3:
Chapters 12–17 (page 41)

1. Atticus and Jem's interaction is one of mutual stubbornness. Scout is used to following Atticus's instructions right away. Atticus tells Jem several times to leave and take Scout home, but Jem adamantly refuses and stays right there.

2. Atticus is not upset. On the way home, Scout sees him reach over and tousle Jem's hair, which Scout says is his one gesture of affection.

3. Atticus is comfortable saying anything he wants in front of Calpurnia because he holds her in high regard and says she knows what she means to the family. He does not see any reason in keeping information from her, especially since she probably already knows it.

4. Scout saves Atticus from the mob through her interaction with Mr. Cunningham. By bringing up personal subjects—his son, Walter, and his legal hassle with entailments—she is able to pull Mr. Cunningham out of the "mob mentality" and put him in Atticus's shoes. He sees Atticus as the father, lawyer, and community member he is instead of just an obstacle to get to Tom Robinson.

Making Connections—Section 3:
Chapters 12–17 (page 42)

1. Scout is afraid of the figures because she thinks they are some sort of "hoodoo" doll (voodoo).

2. Students' responses will vary.

During-Reading Vocabulary Activity—Section 4:
Chapters 18–24 (page 46)

1. Mayella feels **mollified** because Judge Taylor assures her that Atticus will not scare her and the judge is there to help and protect her.

2. Tom's **temerity** to feel sorry for Mayella makes the jurors and other court spectators angry. Even if Mayella is considered "white trash," she is still white and to be pitied by an African American is unacceptable.

Close Reading the Literature—Section 4:
Chapters 18–24 (page 51)

1. There is no evidence in this case; there is simply Mayella's and Mr. Ewell's testimony against Tom Robinson's. No doctor is called for medical evidence and there are no other witnesses.

2. Mayella lies because she broke a code of society and felt ashamed. She kissed Tom, and her father saw. Rather than face the consequences of her actions, she chooses to lie in the hopes that Tom will be convicted and sent to prison. The text says that, like a child, she is attempting to remove the evidence of her wrong-doing.

3. The Ewells think their testimonies will not be doubted simply because they are white. Their prejudices are so deep they feel no one will believe an African American over them.

4. The phrase, "All men are created equal" is false because not all men are born with the same intelligence, wealth, or opportunity. However, it is true because in the eyes of the law and in the court system, each person should be treated equally.

Making Connections—Section 4:
Chapters 18–24 (page 52)

clothing	starched dresses, slips	jeans, dresses
hobbies and interests	church activities, dolls, sewing	sports, crafts
chores	cooking, cleaning	cooking, cleaning
career	nurse, teacher	doctor, engineer

Close Reading the Literature—Section 5:
Chapters 25–31 (page 61)

1. The current events period does not work well because only the town children have access to the newspaper. The rural children either do not have the paper or only have access to *The Grit Paper*, which is not considered an upstanding and respectable publication by the teacher.

2. Miss Gates describes Germany as a dictatorship, where Hitler persecutes the Jews, a religious people who have been driven from their own land. America, she teaches, is a democracy, where there is no persecution or prejudice.

3. After Tom Robinson's trial, Scout overhears Miss Gates say very prejudicial statements about Tom and African Americans. When Miss Gates teaches that there is no prejudice or persecution in America, Scout realizes this is hypocritical and Miss Gates does not even acknowledge her own racial prejudices.

4. Jem has a strong reaction to the trial because he is still trying to sort through his feelings and reactions to the conviction and all of the aftereffects. Atticus says he's trying to forget it, but what he is really doing is storing it away until he can deal with it.

Comprehension Assessment (pages 67–68)

1. D. an innocent person

2. G. "It's not against the law for a citizen to prevent a crime, which is exactly what he [Boo] did."

3. Main Idea: Do the right thing, even if you know the result will be tough.

4. Supporting Details: A. Atticus can't win, but he is able to keep the jury deliberating for a long time. D. Tom Robinson is a guilty man the moment Mayella Ewell opens her mouth and screams.

5. E. People are often blind to their own prejudices.

6. B. "Jem, how can you hate Hitler so bad an' then turn around and be ugly about folks right at home . . . ."

7. The cycle of prejudice is far from over. It has happened in the past, the trial's verdict proves it is still happening, and Atticus is afraid it will continue in the future. Atticus thinks only a child's unprejudiced mind is upset over the injustice.

8. E. "Things haven't caught up with that one's instinct yet. Let him get a little older and he won't get sick and cry."